BEATON

BEATON

Edited and with Text by James Danziger

An Owl Book
Henry Holt and Company
New York

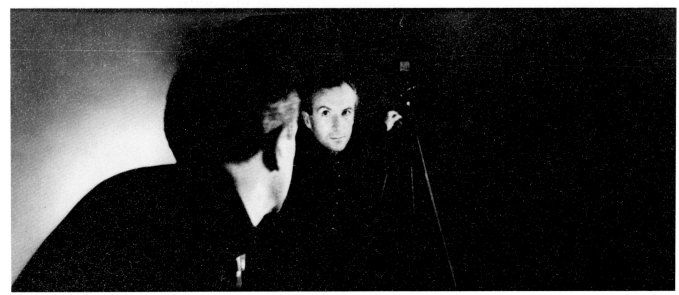

Self-portrait, 1938.

Published by Henry Holt and Company,
521 Fifth Avenue, New York, New York 10175.

Library of Congress Catalog Card Number: 86-045038

ISBN 0-8050-0024-0 (pbk.)

First published in hardcover by Viking Books in 1980
First Owl Book Edition — 1986

Printed in Hong Kong
10 9 8 7 6 5 4 3 2 1

Set in Baskerville.

Frontispiece photo by Helmut Newton.

ISBN 0-8050-0024-0

CONTENTS

PREFACE

I n many years' time, when historians and critics come to give their definitive consideration of Sir Cecil Beaton's achievements, I have no doubt that as a diarist he will be found to have few peers. His drawings and watercolors will be eagerly sought, and the influence of his stage design will linger. I am equally certain that it is as a photographer that his reputation and work will live after him with the significance reserved for great artists.

In the preparation of this book, I have seen virtually every photograph that Beaton ever took, and what impressed me most was not the quality of his work (which I came to take for granted) but the range and chronology of it. Not only was Beaton a master of many genres of photography, he was also a forerunner of many of the aesthetic developments of the medium. In his war pictures, his travel pictures, and the little oddments that crop up regularly through the years, there is an intuitive understanding of the medium and a desire to take pictures within the particular perspective of the camera that have really only begun to be appreciated in the last few years.

The photographs in this book are not only a visual record of one man's times; they are also an account of the development of an artist and a person. Whereas most creative people can be said to have produced their best work during one particular period of their lives, this was not the case with Beaton. He always strove to improve, to be in touch, to stretch himself. It was often a struggle, but in the end he always succeeded.

In my text, I have tried to relate the history of the times and Beaton's own ups and downs to the photographs. I hope by this to show what might have inspired many of the pictures. Other more superficial details are intended simply to add to the enjoyment of looking at a group of pictures which show the unique skill, and more, of one man.

I am indebted to Sir Cecil and to his secretary, Eileen Hose, for all the help and hospitality they have shown me in the years since 1976 when I first met and interviewed Sir Cecil. I am also grateful to Sotheby Parke Bernet for providing the majority of prints reproduced in this book, and to Jocelyn Kargere for the two recent photographs that appeared in French *Vogue*.

A collection of this kind cannot be put together without the help of many people, and I would like to thank, above all, Philippe Garner, of Sotheby's, whose knowledge and enthusiasm have contributed a great deal to this book. I would also like to thank those involved in the book's production: my editor, Olga Zaferatos; Michael Shroyer, the designer; and Barbara Burn, all of Viking Studio books; John Sterling for all his help, together with Kathy Pohl, Adrienne Showering, Nicola Redway, and Hilary Allen.

James Danziger

Postcards of Lily Elsie, early 1900s.

THE EARLY YEARS

Cecil Beaton was born on January 14, 1904, to an intellectual generation that lived and flowered in unprecedented proximity. Born in the same year as Beaton were Christopher Isherwood, Graham Greene, and Nancy Mitford. The previous year's births included those of Evelyn Waugh, George Orwell, Kenneth Clark, and Malcolm Muggeridge, and in the three years that followed, the names of Anthony Powell, John Betjeman, and W. H. Auden duly appeared in the lists of births. Of this august group, none was personally unfamiliar to Beaton, and the majority could well have been considered his friends. Yet while their influence contributed much to Beaton's own intellectual development, the greatest significance lies in the circumstance of Beaton's circle of acquaintance. Through his birth and education, the world that Beaton photographed was observed from the inside, and the sense of familiarity and comfort this conveys adds a unique dimension to his pictures. In a medium where reproduction is based on the cold and scientific effect of light on film, the human element is often insignificant. In Beaton's work it comes first.

The generation that Beaton belonged to was described by Waugh as being quite different from its predecessors in both its claim and its right to attention. "Before it has been the younger generation asserting the fact that they have grown up," he wrote; "today the more modest claim of my generation is that we are young."

With youth as their banner, the bright lights and beauties of a generation dominated the taste of their times, and as they grew up, their faces, their moods, and their style were chronicled by Beaton with the care of a family photographer. Today his pictures are not only synonymous with his times, but exist in a separate right—a record of the artistic concerns and pursuits of one man.

In Beaton's own account, his interest in photography began at the age of three, when, nestled close to his mother as she lay in bed reading her post, he caught a glimpse of a picture postcard of a beautiful young woman. The photograph was of Miss Lily Elsie, a popular actress of the time, and the postcard was a common form of publicity. The child was transfixed, and from then on he began to collect all the cards of his heroine that he could locate.

Lily Elsie, early 1900s.

The photography of the time was as much an imitation of salon painting as it was an art of its own, but the reality and the magic of what it could convey captivated Beaton from the start. As he later recalled:

So absorbed did I become in this somewhat stilted and artificial branch of photography that I cherished even its shortcomings. If an actress were caught in some particularly affected attitude, I was enchanted. Because they appeared behind my favourite's head, the out-of-focus blobs of light like frog spawn which misrepresented the sky seen between the leaves of distant trees had a magic quality for me.

Nancy and Baba, "Babes in a Corot Wood," 1915.

Nancy, "A Norfolk Bacchante," 1917.

Even the small stippling marks, the result of the photographer's retouching, enchanted Beaton, and for many years his early pictures bore the same distinctive marks—painted eyelashes, reduced chins and waistlines, smoothed and whitened complexions.

At the age of eleven Beaton was given his first camera, and with the aid of Ninnie, his sister's nurse, he began to photograph. A complacent and unambitious photographer herself, Ninnie became teacher, adviser, and sometime assistant to Cecil. The pictures that each took at the time present a sharp contrast—Ninnie's were clear, clean snapshots of the children, while Cecil's were underexposed, out-of-focus compositions; Ninnie's were titled simply, "All in the Garden" or "Reggie Bathing," while Cecil's bore the more elaborate titles, "Babes in a Corot Wood" and "A Norfolk Bacchante."

Beaton's pictures were distinctive from the start, for whereas most beginners simply point the camera at an object and shoot, Beaton's first images were careful compositions. In "Babes in a Corot Wood" both the symmetry and scale show signs of a deliber-

ation that was to become more pronounced in the years ahead. Within a very short time virtually all the candid aspects of the snapshot were banished as Cecil's sisters, Nancy (the eldest) and Barbara (known as Baba), were photographed in a variety of traditional theatrical poses, dressed in sheets, surrounded by lamps, and forced to hold poses for as much as five minutes at a time. Failure was at least as likely as success, Beaton being inescapably baffled by the finer points of the science of photography.

Cecil and his younger brother Reggie presented a marked contrast in character. (One sign of the initiative of Reggie is that he rarely appears in any of Cecil's pictures.) When the two started school together, although at different levels, Reggie was able to take the new experience in stride, but for the shy and sensitive Cecil, the first day was a nightmare. As Beaton recalled in his book *The Wandering Years*:

> I was not a particularly puny boy, but I was an excellent bait for bullies for I failed to conceal an inner fear that marked me out as

a prospective victim. On the very first morning that Reggie and I set off to the day-school, Heath Mount, Hampstead, I tried not to disclose to my younger brother my dread of the Dickensian cruelty we were probably about to face. As we walked along Hampstead Heath with our emerald green caps and satchels, my stomach was queasy at the prospect of having my knuckles slashed with a sharp ruler by some sadistic master, or my backside swiped until it bled. It was with relief, on that cold autumn morning, that I heard the whistle blow for the eleven o'clock break. Half the morning, at any rate, had passed without disaster. The masters I now knew were not sadistic. Now the entire school was let out to rampage over the asphalt playground. The older boys formed their own posses of interest, others were playing the hearty games continued from last term. All the new boys seemed rather lost and did not know where to go; but none looked more ill at ease than myself. Suddenly, out of nowhere, the bullies arrived. They had recognised their quarry in me. Growling like wire-haired terriers, they were large and solid, with hairy stockings and rough tweeds. Their leader was a boy half the size of the others, wearing Barrie-esque green tweed knickerbockers. Recognising from a distance that I was the most obvious lamb for the slaughter, the leader, having darted silently towards me at great speed, halted a few inches in front of me with a menacing wild stare, while the bigger boys circled me and growled louder. He then stood on his toes and slowly thrust his face with a diabolical stare, closer and closer to mine, ever closer until the eyes converged into one enormous Cyclops nightmare. It was a clever inauguration to the terrors that followed, and my introduction to Evelyn Waugh.

Having survived Waugh and the years at Heath Mount, at the age of thirteen Beaton entered Harrow School. Hearty in its demeanor and conservative in attitude, the school did not provide much opportunity or encouragement for photography, especially of the theatrical variety to which Cecil was inclined, and whenever a willing model and accomplice was found, a furtive disposition was as important a quality as a photogenic appearance.

One morning, Cecil and a friend decided to risk taking pictures in the housemaster's garden. Rising early, they took turns striking classical poses among the shrubbery, each boy startlingly arrayed in Greco-Roman draperies. Engrossed in their artistic pursuits, the boys did not see the faces that began to

*Cecil (*right*), age eight, and Reggie.*

Mr. and Mrs. Ernest Beaton, 1918.

Baba, Nancy, and their cousin, Tecia Chattock.

appear at windows throughout the house. When the morning light awoke her, the housemaster's wife rose to draw the curtains and was greeted by the sight of two half-naked bodies. She called her husband to witness the display, and together they stood watching in amazement. When the young Beaton finally looked up, he saw with horror a silent audience of boys, who, as soon as Beaton and his friend started to bolt, greeted them with hoots of derision.

From then on photography became limited to holidays until the day when Beaton acquired an accessory called the "Automatic Self-Portrait Release." When a lever on this device was pressed, a clockwork delay with a loud metallic buzz was activated, continuing for twenty or thirty seconds until the shutter clicked. "It was a cold-blooded and slightly sinister procedure, and I would become acutely embarrassed if ever caught in the act of self-photography," Beaton wrote, "but by the time I was eighteen, I had learnt much about the effects of lights placed at given positions on my own face."

Together with a careful analysis of the photographs in fashion magazines, these experiments constituted Beaton's apprenticeship. His mentor, although distant in miles, was the great Baron de Meyer, whose soft-focus photographs had defined the style of the early 1900s. To imitate the incandes-

cent light that surrounded the Baron's subjects, Beaton's *modus operandi* included the use of as many as six dressing-table mirrors, each angled carefully to reflect a small patch of light from one window, back and forth around the sitter.

Clumsy though these methods were, Beaton's pictures achieved a consistent purpose and quality. His concern was to fabricate something of the fantasy world he longed for from the materials at hand, and in his pictures of his mother and sisters he had become adept at disguising the homespun origin of his props with ingenious sophistication. Sheets became medieval costumes, carpets became robes, and a blurred background effect was achieved by instructing the sister who was not being photographed to shake a rug behind the other.

By the time he was seventeen, Beaton's photographs were proficient examples of the pictorial genre, and his ambitions at the time were to exhibit his photographs in the Royal Photographic Society's salons and to have them published in the local newspaper. To this end he persuaded one sitter after another to pose in the middle of his ingenious arrangements. He scoured the secondhand shops and theatrical design studios for backgrounds and props, and toiled late into the night in his makeshift darkroom.

Early attempt at self-portraiture, 1920.

Mrs. Ernest Beaton, "a perfect Madonna."

Nancy, "looking very Spanish and absolutely perfect," 1921.

The entries in Beaton's diaries give a vivid impression of the routine, the hazards, and the experimentation involved in his early photography.

Instead of going to see Pavlova, I spent the evening enlarging. I enlarged quite a lot of that perfect Madonna one of Mama, but I did not get a perfect print. I was rather annoyed. I went on enlarging and it got so late and then at about 12 o'clock a terrible thing happened. I was holding the standard lamp to look at a print in the acid when the wire knocked a huge china basin full of acid over me and the carpet, and the basin smashed into a thousand bits. I got into a panic. I tidied the room as best I could and swamped the floor and carpet with water, and I scrubbed and swabbed with a nail brush. I put my trousers (luckily old flannel ones) in a basin of water. I was exhausted and came downstairs and ate some plums.

There is one simply splendid picture I have taken of Nancy looking very Spanish and absolutely perfect. I printed it with a layer of glass between the negative and the paper to give it a soft-focus effect. The result is terribly beautiful although nothing like

Nancy. The texture of the lace, skin, and fringe on shawl is perfect, and I spend my entire time looking at it. It is frightfully reminiscent of a picture taken by Goya and it is terribly interesting, although it is not the best photograph I have taken as the picture is severely spoilt by a knee sticking up high and making it look as if Nancy is riding side-saddle. I showed the picture to that horrid little Pleydell-Bingham who sniggered and said it was like Lady Diana Cooper. What an ordinary stupid remark! I'd like to kick the little man! Such a little tick.

The sun came out and I was making the best of my printing time. I became very excited over a new method of printing I've invented which gives the most perfect results. I half print a photograph through a thickness of glass and it makes the print all blurred; then for the other half of its printing time I print it sharp on the blurred image so that the effect is marvellously soft as well as detailed.

Beaton left Harrow with a reputation for being "artistic." He showed some talent in drawing and had produced some highly original photographs, yet he was totally unsure what to make of his future. Aware of his son's lack of confidence, Ernest Beaton set off for Cambridge, and barely a month before the start of the academic year, he managed to charm the Master of St. John's College into securing a place for Cecil.

On October 4, 1922, Cecil Beaton arrived at Cambridge. His timing was impeccable, for the Oxford and Cambridge of the twenties were the twin temples of aestheticism. Beaton's contemporaries were celebrated for their youth and unconventionality; they were individually recognizable models from whom such writers as Evelyn Waugh and Anthony Powell were to draw their characters.

Walking arm in arm through the colleges, the students flaunted a naïvely exhibitionist brand of homosexuality. At Oxford, John Betjeman was known for carrying a yellow teddy bear with him wherever he went, and Harold Acton first achieved notoriety by inventing "bags"—trousers as wide as twenty-six inches at the ankle. Shortly after his arrival at Cambridge, Beaton was wearing a scarlet tie, gauntlet gloves, a long medieval robe, and flowing hair, and although the prototypical young aesthete

was more correctly assumed to be an Oxford man, the Cambridge student, not to be outdone, made an effort to be equally flamboyant, equally passionate, and equally outrageous. Rooms were decorated with antiques and fine paintings, yet in spite of a climate so apparently conducive to his inclinations, Beaton did not shine. His shyness, together with a certain lack of purpose, inhibited him from making the grand gestures necessary to establish himself as a personality. He disdained academics, made few friends, and if it had not been for his interest in dramatics, it is doubtful that much would have survived to link his name with that era.

As it was, his pictures of various Cambridge players came to the eye of Dorothy Todd, then editor of British *Vogue,* and in 1924 a portrait titled "The Duchess of Malfi" was published in the magazine. In reality, the picture was taken outside the gentlemen's lavatory in the theater lobby, and the figure was George Rylands, a friend of Beaton's, who was taking the title role in a Marlowe Dramatic Society production; nevertheless, the words "Photograph by Beaton" appeared under the picture, and for his work he received the then princely sum of thirty shillings.

Ernest Beaton, Nancy, Reggie, Mrs. Beaton, and Cecil, 1921.

George Rylands as the "Duchess of Malfi," Cambridge, 1924.

Boy Lebas, Cambridge, 1922.

As little as he gained academically, however, the years at Cambridge did force Beaton to become more independent. After a weekend visit by his parents, he wrote in his diary:

> I walked Mama to the University Arms Hotel and said goodbye. I felt rather brutal when I realised I didn't mind going back to my rooms alone. What a change! I can remember the time when I cried in bed at night because my governess told me that in Heaven people's shapes were different. I didn't want my mother to assume another shape.

Cecil's interests, which were limited to art, society, and theater, served furthermore only to alienate him from his father. A lunch he wrote of the next day was "rather startling."

> My father kept asking me awful questions about Cambridge—questions that were impossible to answer. He asked questions like this: How many St. John's people are there in the rugger fifteen? How many St. John's people in the cricket eleven? I don't know any of these things. I don't even know the names of the athletes. To crown it all, my father asked what the St. John's colours were. I was covered with confusion.

After three years at Cambridge Beaton left without taking a degree. He had become a self-avowed snob, and a lost soul, and was once again in a position of complete uncertainty as to his future.

At home in London the family timber company, once successful enough to keep the Beatons in style, had not prospered, and the American side of the business had been lost to a competitor. As the situation worsened, the family was forced to move from Hyde Park Street to a smaller house in Sussex Gardens, and the Beaton boys became accountable for themselves. Cecil was now twenty, and his younger brother Reggie had already been at work in the city for a year.

At first Cecil tried to hold his own by taking on photographic commissions, but the work was scarce, and to Beaton's father the occasional assignment seemed little more than an excuse for remaining unemployed. After putting up with it for a few months, he sent Cecil to work in his office. Cecil was given an accounting job, but his mathematics was so poor and his handwriting so unsuited to the task (having been styled from the age of five in imitation of Lily Elsie's) that at the end of a month a new man had to be hired to find Cecil's mistakes.

His father gave him permission to take up photography again, and Cecil built up orders for portraits. But when the commissions began to dwindle, Cecil was sent back to work in the City. With Reggie now working successfully in timber, Cecil was put in the employ of Mr. Schmiegelow, a Danish friend of his father's, who was in the cement business. This job, which consisted of typing the company's letters, turned out to be a great improvement, for Mr. Schmiegelow would often give Cecil the afternoon off to show his work to magazines. However, he met with rejection after rejection, and by 1926 Beaton was to write in his diary:

> My God—June the first! None of my visits to publishers have come to anything so I've cheapened myself for nothing. At Cambridge I used to have such a high opinion of myself and now I see what a snob I am. Even in my most sincere moments I harbour absurd and petty notions about fame. It all leads to nothing, only everlasting disappointment. Perhaps I am after wrong and impossible things—that is very likely true. Yet I want these things, I should like these unreal things to happen. I'm twenty-two years old. Yet I know that I'm talented in many ways—and I've got a tremendous personality. Something must *must* happen.

In desperation Beaton wrote to the BBC offering his services as a commentator. He received a reply summoning him to an audition, and on the appointed day, fearful and with a severe cold and running nose, he arrived at BBC headquarters.

When the interviewer asked him to speak into a microphone, Beaton began to recite from a story he had written at Cambridge, but after a few short paragraphs he was asked to stop. "It's no use," said the BBC interviewer. "Does a cold make a difference?" asked Cecil. The interviewer agreed that it could, but explained to Beaton just why his voice would be unsuitable. The BBC considered their listeners to be "the masses." Since "the masses" were predominantly lower middle class, it followed that it would not do to have someone whose accent would sound too patronizing. To clarify the explanation, the interviewer imitated Beaton's voice, and the result was enough to make Beaton sick. "Why, I talked just like the silly ass in musical comedy," he wrote, "the one with spats, large buttonhole, and eyeglass."

Disillusioned, Beaton returned to the gentle monotony of Schmiegelow's office, but at the end of August the banality of his routine was broken by an invitation to tag along with two professional journalists who were going to Italy to report on Baroness d'Erlanger's costume ball, the social event of the

In his room at Cambridge, 1922.

Self-portrait, 1923.

Left to right: *Rex Whistler, Beaton, Georgia Sitwell, William Walton, Stephen Tennant, Zita Jungman, and Tessa Jungman at Cambridge, 1923.*

Venetian calendar. With his father's permission, Cecil set off for Venice, joining the throngs of working photographers, who eyed him suspiciously as he clutched his little Kodak. The amateurishness of his methods that was fast becoming his trademark was appalling. When one society matron posed for him, his tripod slipped all over the marble floor. When he was photographing another, his intense seriousness and his demand for unusual poses made her unable to stop laughing.

A few days later a mutual friend introduced Beaton to Sergei Diaghilev, the famous impresario of the Ballets Russes. The dominant figure of twentieth-century aestheticism, Diaghilev was a friend to Satie, Picasso, Cocteau, and Gide, and when he agreed to review Beaton's portfolio, Beaton felt himself to be at one of the crossroads of his life. Looking at various drawings, set designs, and photographs, Diaghilev commented on each. When he came to a

photograph of Nancy and Baba, their image reflected against a shiny table, he stopped. "I like this. It is very curious," he said. From then on Diaghilev's concentration was given solely to the photographs.

The encouragement fired Beaton with resolution, and when he returned to London, it was with the determination to resign from Mr. Schmiegelow's office. His father acknowledged the futility of the connection and granted his son permission to leave. On September 7, 1926, Cecil went to say good-bye to his employer. They talked about careers and ambition and Cecil's hope that one day his father would understand his motivation. Mr. Schmiegelow promised to do his best to explain this, but before Cecil left, he let him in on a secret. "Don't ever repeat it," he warned, "but all the time you have been here, your father has been paying me the one pound a week I pay you. He knows you'll never be a businessman—he just wants you to be disciplined."

Nancy and Baba, 1924.

Daphne du Maurier, 1926.

THE STUDIO AT SUSSEX GARDENS

The house in Sussex Gardens now became Beaton's studio, and as his reputation began to grow, people flocked in to have their pictures taken. At the beginning the sitters were mostly debutantes and friends from the university, but as time passed, more prominent people arrived.

What distinguished Beaton's work at this time was a natural flair for flattering portraiture, together with a strong sense of the correct relationship between the sitter, the costume, and the background. While all these elements had figured strongly in Beaton's earlier work, the sureness and dramatic impact that he was achieving by the late 1920s were a new development.

In "Debutantes of 1927" what seems an effective but simple composition was in reality the result of much planning and labor. The background was painted by Beaton from a detail of "The Swing" by Fragonard, and the flowers held by the girls were precisely arranged around the figures to pick up the floral motif of the background, combining the real and artificial with skill. (The inevitable Beaton blunder is also visible—the back of a dressing table mirror, used to reflect light, shows at the bottom of the frame.)

Soon Edith Sitwell, the avant-garde poet and sister of the famous Sitwell brothers, Osbert and Sacheverell, came to be photographed, and Cyril Connolly, an old friend and already a successful author, reappeared to spend the afternoon in a variety of poses. At times the second floor room that Cecil used as his studio became so crowded it was impossible for people to move about. Women in various stages of décolleté, sitting around ready to be photographed, gave the room the appearance of a girls' dormitory. Daphne du Maurier declared it resembled a brothel. In spite of this Beaton's photographs were becoming more original, and less imitative of the work of his early heroes. Aware of the difference, Beaton wrote in his diary: "Till now my pictures have been ordinary attempts to make people look as beautiful as possible, but these are fantastic and amusing. They strike me as being an achievement."

Beaton's painted backgrounds—some romantic, others art deco in style—were works of art in themselves; so were the illusory settings that were beginning to appear in his work. People were photographed with their heads under glass domes. They

"Debutantes of 1927": (left to right) Lady Georgina Curzon, Lady Anne Wellesley, Miss Deirdre Hart-Davis, and Miss Nancy Beaton.

were wrapped in silver cloth or posed like statues. A photograph of Margot Asquith, Lady Oxford, taken from behind, was immediately caricatured by Evelyn Waugh in his first novel, *Decline and Fall.* David Lennox, the society photographer "who for three years had never been known to give anyone a complimentary sitting," is described as having taken "two eloquent portraits of the back of Margot Beste-Chetwynde's head and one of the reflection of her hands in a bowl of ink."

In spite of Waugh's satiric tone, the unconventionality of Beaton's photographs was always effective, and the props he used were never allowed to detract from the importance of the sitter. Above all, his pictures were modern, a fact instinctively seized upon by the Sitwells, and Edith in particular became one of Beaton's most frequent models and an accomplice in many of his most dramatic and theatrical tableaux.

The importance of the Sitwells' patronage was enormous. They were influential, aristocratic, and

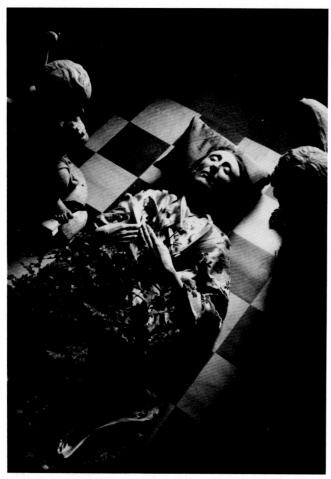

Edith Sitwell, 1927.

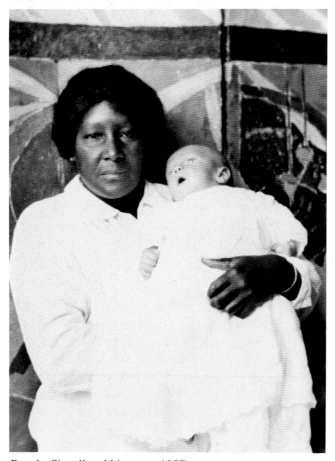

Reresby Sitwell and his nurse, 1927.

the *enfants terribles* of the new generation. Edith Sitwell had achieved notoriety when, at her first poetry recital, she had read her latest work through a megaphone from behind a screen. Her brothers, who proclaimed themselves great writers, reveled in disdaining the status quo and reaping the resulting publicity. Together, their self-appointed task was to shock the complacent and bring a sense of enthusiasm and vitality to the English world of arts and letters. Beaton's photographs reflected all that the Sitwells stood for, and they in turn complemented his work to perfection.

By 1928 Beaton was flourishing financially and socially. Now that his concerns regarding happiness and security were appeased, he was free to concentrate his energy on work. By the end of the year he had decided that the time had come for him to have his first one-man show, and having found a gallery willing to exhibit his work, Beaton approached Osbert Sitwell to write an introduction to the catalogue.

Osbert's "Appreciation," as it was called, turned out to be a witty and stylish piece of writing, as well as a perceptive and intelligent analysis of Beaton's photography. "The desire to be photographed," he wrote, "is certainly as old as the legend of Narcissus." He continued:

Mr. Cecil Beaton is now the stern nemesis who transmutes his various sitters into so many flowers, simple or orchidaceous. As a photographer, his methods are relentless, he must needs be cruel to be kind—that is to say that, though the sitters are certainly "put through it," the result justifies the means. Mr. Beaton is a photographic pioneer, and just as one other noted explorer, dropping all the paraphernalia of equatorial suits and sunhats, marched through the central forest of Brazil with bowler, umbrella and blue serge suit, so, in the perilous voyage toward his discoveries, Mr. Cecil Beaton is armed with naught save a ladder, a tripod and a Kodak. The exquisite photographs he produces are the fruit of the simplest of all photographic machines, while he himself executes the most dangerous poses, worthy of a Blondin or of a Ducalion, balanced at the very summit of a rickety ladder. Under these circumstances it is natural that there should be accidents, and so damaged is the Kodak, which is even now in its present state as full of magic as Aladdin's Lamp, that it has to be covered in a sad case of pink tulle, to protect it and to prevent the light from filtering in. Indeed, one of the most terrifying incidents I

The Sitwell family. Left to right: *Sacheverell, Sir George, Georgia, Reresby, Lady Ida, Edith, and Osbert.*

have witnessed in a lifetime of adventure was on the occasion that my sister, my brother and myself were lying at full length on the floor waiting to be photographed, when suddenly the whole world rocked and Mr. Beaton and the ladder and Kodak were wrecked with us in an inextricable confusion.

The peculiar excellence of Mr. Beaton's photographs is that they are so photographic—he never tries to make them into pictures or statues. . . . Who has ever seen Lady Oxford look more like Lady Oxford? The bustle and tenuous figure against a cubist background sum up the achievements of a considerable lifetime. The quiet and gentle sophistication of Miss Baba Beaton strikes a new note in beauty. Here we have faces that in the next few years will assuredly launch a thousand ships, and should be preserved to maintain our ratio against America—a suggestion towards economy that one would like to make to the Admiralty. And if the race of mortals were to perish from this earth, and nothing remain of the wreck except a few of Mr. Cecil Beaton's photographs, there is no doubt that those beings who succeed us would pronounce this past set as one of extraordinary beauty.

As the time of the exhibition drew near, more and more people found the time and inclination to drop by Beaton's studio for a last-minute sitting, and in the rush everybody in the Beaton family was put to work. The butler became a lighting assistant, Ninnie was put in charge of the invitations, and it was not until the day of the opening that everything was in its place. The only threat to the day was the weather—a pea-soup fog had enveloped London, and visibility was limited so seriously that traffic had come to a standstill all through the city. In spite of this, by lunchtime the gallery was reasonably crowded. By late afternoon it was packed. The public flocked to see the highly unconventional pictures of Lady Milbanke and the Sitwells, Lady Oxford, and William Walton. The popular newspapers fought each other for exclusive rights to the pictures, and before long, having one's picture taken by Cecil Beaton became a public catch phrase.

If the years at Cambridge had failed to live up to their romantic promise, the years that followed redressed the balance with a vengeance. Beaton's face appeared regularly in the society columns of the newspapers. As a result of his newly found fame, his productivity swelled to include writing articles in which he offered his distinctive opinion of fashion and people in the news. The friends he now made were either prominent or full of promise, and his

Rex Whistler, 1936.

days were busy from his waking hour onward. His career had taken off, and the pages of his diaries are filled with fleeting images of lunches with the Sitwells, costume parties with the Guinnesses, and cocktails with Rex Whistler, the young illustrator and designer.

As Beaton enjoyed himself, he made influential connections, and on one of her yearly visits to England Mrs. Edna Chase, the editor of American *Vogue,* was introduced to Beaton and his photography. "Obviously amateur, but personal and interesting," was her judgment. Her curiosity piqued, she visited Beaton at his home. When she was shown the bathroom/developing room and introduced to Ninnie, the darkroom technician, her astonishment was complete, but she was not dismayed. Before she left England, she called Cecil and offered him an open and noncommittal invitation: if he ever came to New York, she would love to have him do some work for her.

To Cecil, the very idea of New York was a stimulant. It was 1929, and America was still very much the New World. In Beaton's imagination his transatlantic success was inevitable. A quick trip was irresistible, and in November 1929 Beaton set sail for New York.

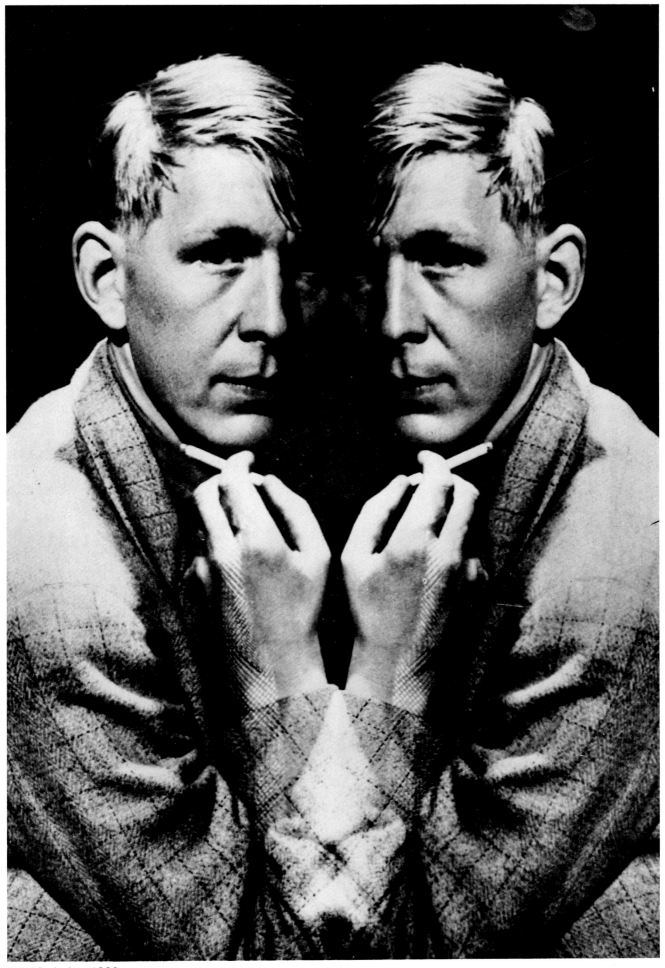

W. H. Auden, 1930.

Fred and Adele Astaire in the apartment of Condé Nast, 1930.

AMERICA

Armed with a sheaf of introductions from his London friends, Beaton took a room in the Ambassador Hotel on Park Avenue and 55th Street, as respectable a hotel as he could afford, and waited for the first replies to his letters. He had brought with him two hundred pounds (nearly one thousand dollars at that time) to tide him over until he gained his first commissions.

By Christmas the few commissions he had managed to obtain far from balanced his expenditures, and in January, when Beaton attended a party given by Mrs. Harrison Williams he had only twenty dollars—his entire capital—in his pocket. His hostess, he was told, was worth two hundred million dollars! Through the talk of bull and bear markets, stock quotations, and hundred-dollar golf bets, she noticed the eccentrically dressed and by now desperately awkward young man from England and found time to have a word with him. She found him sympathetic, and by the end of the evening Cecil was able to feel he had made an important friend.

In the weeks that followed, his intuition was proved correct. Along with Mrs. Williams, Mrs. Dodge-Sloan, Mrs. Walter C. Rosen, Mrs. Morton Schwartz, and Mrs. Shevlin Smith all found time to be photographed, and soon Beaton was making enough money not only to feed himself but to rent the hotel room adjoining his for use as a studio.

After acquiring the sort of backdrops and props that satisfied him, the only foreseeable barrier to Beaton's success lay in the field of photographic processing. (The results of one too many sittings had been ruined by the crudity of drugstore processing.) The technical details of printing were, however, solved with the discovery of an old Russian immigrant who took care of the film with the delicacy of an artist.

The finished prints pleased the sitters. When they were shown to Mrs. Chase at *Vogue,* she was sufficiently impressed to bring them to the attention of Condé Nast. Before long, Beaton was taking pictures in Mr. Nast's luxurious penthouse of Fred and Adele Astaire, Gertrude Lawrence, and other celebrities, and in spite of the primitive equipment he persisted in using, his work was immediately published.

Years later Alfred Lunt and Lynn Fontanne recalled how the Beaton of their first meeting trembled with shyness and waged a continuous war against his

Alfred Lunt and Lynn Fontanne, 1930.

tripod. He climbed ladders to gain an unusual point of view, held his breath during the long exposures, yet the results pleased them more than any pictures of them taken previously.

Surprisingly, though, as the financial and social rewards came pouring in, Beaton did not see himself remaining a photographer for long. At a New York exhibition of his work, held in the showroom of interior designer Elsie de Wolfe, Beaton insisted on displaying drawings and watercolors, and one sketch—drawn in art class at Harrow—was sold to a Mr. Ralph Beaver Strassberger for a thousand dollars!

Before his trip was over, Beaton had signed a contract with Condé Nast to take pictures exclusively for *Vogue* at a salary of several thousand pounds a year. When he left New York after six months, Cecil was delighted to find his cabin overflowing with flowers, telegrams, and champagne sent by friends and admirers.

As coincidence would have it, bound for England on the same ship was Noel Coward. Although

With Oliver Messel and Mogens Tuede (top) and Mrs. Harrison Williams.

the two had never met, Coward was justifiably hostile as the result of several unflattering pieces Beaton had written about him in his occasional columns, but by the end of the voyage they had patched up their differences.

It was an interesting and revealing friendship, for although similar in many ways, in terms of the image each presented to the public they differed completely—the conservative and guarded Coward mistrusted the superficial instinct of people, while the more liberal Beaton displayed by his very flamboyance a certain trust in the good nature of his fellow man. He recorded Coward's advice to him in his diary:

"It is important not to let the public have a loophole to lampoon you." That he explained was why he studied his own facade. Now take his voice: it was definite, harsh, rugged. He moved firmly and solidly, dressed quietly. "You should appraise yourself," he went on, "your sleeves are too tight, your voice is too high and too precise. You mustn't do it. It closes so many doors. It limits you unnecessarily, and young men with half your intelligence will laugh at you." He shook his head, wrinkled his forehead, and added disarmingly, "It's hard, I know. One would like to indulge one's own taste. I myself dearly love a good match, yet I know it is overdoing it to wear a tie, socks, and handkerchief of the same colour. I take ruthless stock of myself in the mirror before going out, for even a polo jumper or unfortunate tie exposes one to danger."

Back in London once again, Beaton became increasingly aware of his growing reputation and independence, and decided that the next logical step for him was to put together a book.

The contents were quickly drawn from the best of his portraits, and, together with a brief text, the project was presented to Duckworth Publishers. It was immediately accepted, and within a few months a limited edition of the book appeared. Titled *The Book of Beauty,* it consisted of photographs and sketches of the well-known beauties of the day, accompanied by an extraordinarily gushing prose. Its success was instant, and Emerald Cunard, who was arguably the most important woman socially in London, astonished her lunch guests one day by throwing the book into the fire and running it through with a red-hot poker. "He's a low fellow, and it's a terrible book," she screamed after seeing herself described as a "hostess," an ambiguously flattering word for the time.

While the book's very exclusivity was bound to arouse interest, its real merits lay much deeper. By 1930 Beaton was working with the freedom of imagination to break existing convention, and while the word "surreal" was often applied to his work, the proper definition served to exclude him. Aware of this, Beaton was not anxious to be included in the movement, for whereas surrealism sought to explore the subconscious aspects of the mind, Beaton's pictures chose to deal with the more conscious realms of daydreams and fantasies. In spite of this his pictures of women, while idealized representations on one hand, also showed them to be strong and emancipated personalities.

Lily Elsie, from The Book of Beauty, *1930.*

Joan Crawford, 1931.

THE THIRTIES

In 1931 Beaton made his first trip to Hollywood and was instantly smitten by the town. The great movie stars, who until then he had seen only on celluloid, posed eagerly, inspiring Beaton most uncharacteristically to put aside the chasteness of his normal work to convey the sex appeal on which such stars as Tallulah Bankhead, Joan Crawford, Dolores Del Rio, and Johnny Weissmuller depended.

In another series of pictures Beaton used the stark setting of the backlots, where lighting beams and half-constructed sets made up the background. These settings, so original at the time, were so effective that twenty years later they were being carefully followed by experts in still photography.

The only star whom Beaton failed to photograph was the person he most wanted to—Greta Garbo. Yet, no matter how hard he and the MGM publicity department tried to persuade her, she remained aloof. "He talks to newspapers," was one comment that Garbo reportedly made.

A year later, just before Beaton's next visit to Hollywood was about to end, Eddie Goulding, a friend who had directed Garbo in *Grand Hotel,* was able to effect an introduction. Beaton's first glimpse of Garbo is described in his diary in magical terms. He was taking a nap in Goulding's house and woke to hear voices in the garden below. "If a unicorn had suddenly appeared in the late afternoon light of this ugly, ordinary garden, I could have been neither more surprised nor more amazed by the beauty of this exotic creature," he wrote.

He came down to meet her and was overcome with shyness, but as the evening progressed, they began to talk easily. When it was time for her to leave, Beaton felt as though his dream were about to be destroyed. "Can I lunch with you tomorrow?" he pleaded.

"No," was her reply.

"Shall we meet again?"

"No."

In desperation Beaton grabbed hold of a feather duster that lay on the sofa next to where she sat. "Can I keep this as a memento?"

"No."

"Then this is good-bye."

"Yes, I'm afraid so. *C'est la vie!*"

Back in England in 1933 the Beaton family was in a state of flux. Nancy was married, Baba had become engaged, and Reggie had joined the Royal Air Force.

On October 16 the family was informed that Reggie had been killed by an underground train: he had fallen onto the tracks and had been crushed to death. At the inquest the coroner passed a verdict of suicide, and the judgment left the entire family shattered.

Barely a year later Beaton reached the age of thirty. His home was now in Wiltshire, but he spent much of his time traveling through Europe. In 1935, after meetings with Picasso, Cocteau, Cartier-Bresson, and Gertrude Stein, Beaton recorded the death of his father in the pages of his diary. The long period of his youth had ended.

With Anita Loos at San Simeon, California, 1931.

Photograph by George Platt Lynes, 1938.

THE ROYAL YEARS

In Britain the year 1936 was ushered in with the ascent of King Edward VIII. In one of Beaton's scrapbooks from that time, among the newspaper clippings and snapshots, he included a piece of blue stationery. Dated October 1936, it is the record of a bet made with Juliet Duff: "I, Juliet Duff, bet Cecil Beaton five pounds (¡5) that His Majesty King Edward VIII will be married to Mrs. Simpson before October 25, 1937."

It was not a surprising wager for him to make. He was aware that the press reports concerning the King and Mrs. Simpson had been withheld from the British public. He had met Wallis Simpson many times and had taken her photograph. When on one occasion he lightheartedly informed her of his bet and suggested that it might ruin him, Mrs. Simpson replied, "No, I expect I'll be very poor and that you'll clean up."

A month later the British press ended its silence, and on December 11 King Edward broke the news of his abdication to his people. Within hours Edward, no longer His Majesty but now His Royal Highness, was bound for France on board H.M.S. *Fury*. The circle of Beaton's friends who had rejoiced in the implication of a young and fun-loving King now reeled under the psychological blow of his successor's accession, for George VI was as down-to-earth and conservative as his brother was flamboyant and apparently progressive.

Within months of the abdication barely a handful of the Duke of Windsor's old friends cared to acknowledge their former ties, inspiring Osbert Sitwell to write a poem titled "Rat Week." Among the friends who remained loyal, the names Duff Cooper, Lady Diana Cooper, Randolph Churchill, and the Sitwells—all Beaton intimates—featured prominently.

In the spring of 1937 Beaton was summoned to France by the Duke of Windsor for the express purpose of taking some photographs of Wallis to counterbalance the unflattering pictures of her that the British press was printing. The Duke wanted her to be seen in a more romantic light, but while Beaton was anxious to comply, the future Duchess's features were not ideally suited to a flowery soft-focus approach. Nevertheless, the photographic session lasted for many hours on the grounds and in the rooms of the Château de Candé, where the couple was staying. One photograph in particular—of Mrs. Simp-

Wallis Simpson, 1937.

son dressed in white against an open doorway—achieved the effect everyone wanted.

One month later, and under conditions of great secrecy, Beaton received another call from France. This time he was requested to take wedding pictures. The pictures, taken the day before the actual ceremony, were among the most important that Beaton had ever produced. Beaton was well aware of the role he had been given in one of the great romantic dramas of his time, and he duly recorded the event in his diary:

> Wallis hovered about in yellow, slightly more businesslike than usual, with her face showing the strain; she looked far from her best. The Duke, by contrast, seemed radiant—his hair ruffled gold, his complexion clear and sunburnt, his blue eyes transparent with excitement. Marriage in Westminster Abbey should have been his birthright, yet now he beamed contentedly at the impromptu wedding arrangements set up in a music room.

"Mock Puppet Theatre," 1939.

Christian Bérard with his portrait of Beaton, 1937.

To avoid possible sightseers with telescopic lenses, we had to confine ourselves to shaded parts of the house. As misfortune would have it, Forwood (the Duke's equerry) brought some bad news just as the bridal couple posed at a turret window. Through the lens I saw the Duke become worried, frowning and contorting his face until he looked as tortured as a German gargoyle. Wallis, too, seemed troubled. It was painful. I couldn't very well interrupt and say, "Please look pleasant." I took several illuminating pictures. Then the mood changed for the better again as Wallis suggested, "Let's remember now, we're having our pictures taken."

A few hours later Beaton returned to England, where a week earlier George VI had been crowned King in Westminster Abbey. After the upheaval of the previous months, the country was occupied with putting itself back in order. Intimations of trouble with Germany began to build up, but the average person was content to ignore them.

For Beaton 1937 was a year of carefree travel. At the beginning of the year he took a remarkable series of pictures of New York, then went on to visit Spain, Monaco, Malta, Greece, Turkey, and France. No hint of an awareness of any crisis appeared in Beaton's diaries until late August, and even then it was ironically inappropriate. While his portrait was being painted by the French painter and set designer Christian Bérard, Beaton sensed that Bérard was depressed. In reply to his questions, Bérard showed Beaton his draft notice and explained that what frightened him as much as the thought of war was the knowledge that his induction would entail an unavoidable disintoxication from opium.

During the next few months the public became increasingly confused as events pointed to one conclusion and then another. After Chamberlain's 1938 visit to Munich, Beaton was once again sure that peace would continue. In 1939, in spite of what must have been an inevitable realization of what was to come, Beaton continued his transatlantic journeys.

At Condé Nast's insistence, Beaton reluctantly put aside his pocket Kodak for an 8x10 large-format camera, and although the process of maneuvering the larger camera added to Beaton's discomfort, the results showed a more concise and reflective approach to his subject. His fashion pictures for *Vogue* represented a new apex in his career.

The change can be seen at once in Beaton's contact prints, for whereas his early pictures used only a small part of the negative, the borders being determined after printing, by the late 1930s his fashion

Her Majesty Queen Elizabeth The Queen Mother, 1939.

photographs tended to take up the whole frame. While a photograph like "Debutantes of 1927" was indeed carefully staged, two of the girls' expressions—blurred and surprised—betray an unintentional candidness. In the mock puppet theater picture of 1939 the posing, the expression, and the composition are totally deliberate.

The fashion pictures of the 1930s retained Beaton's thematic concerns with art and artifice, but at the same time, he was becoming a master of the practical necessities of his trade. The purpose of his photographs was to show clothes, and no matter how elaborate the conception, he never failed to fulfill this obligation. As a result, he was rarely out of work.

On July 12, 1939, Beaton returned from his working trip to the States. He had not been in his house an hour before he received a call from Buck-

ingham Palace. A lady-in-waiting wanted to know if Beaton could photograph the Queen the next day. Once assured that the call was not a practical joke, Beaton accepted with alacrity. In view of Beaton's reputation for unconventionality and the Queen's antipathy to all people socially or temperamentally allied with the Duke and Duchess of Windsor, the summons was exceptionally impressive.

To help justify the Queen's selection of Beaton as the photographer, the next morning he shaved with extra care and put on his most conservative suit and tie. At the Palace he was met by a courtier who told him that the Queen wanted to discuss with him the dresses she would wear.

"Like all courtiers, this particular gentleman appeared to assume an air of slight stagefright at the mention of royalty," wrote Beaton, "and this successfully infected me with a becoming nervousness. We

Her Majesty Queen Elizabeth The Queen Mother, 1939.

looked grave, as if we were expecting news of a severe illness, or some other disaster, while we waited a moment outside the door of the Queen's study."
Once the choice of clothing had been made, the picture taking went without a hitch. For Beaton, a photographic session was either a complete disaster or a great success. That day every tripod stayed in place, every light worked perfectly, and the poses all came naturally.

After Beaton had spent several hours with the Queen, an attendant whispered to Beaton that because of the length of the session the King was being forced to have his tea alone. Still the Queen continued. Pictures were taken in the various state rooms, in the Palace gardens, and by the lake. When King George finally saw the result of the garden pictures,

with the Queen a solitary figure in party dress, holding a frilly parasol, he dubbed the picture "The Unsuccessful Hostess."

Only the fading daylight caused the Queen to stop, but by that time Beaton had established himself as an approved court photographer. This was enough to make Beaton the best-known photographer in the land, yet in spite of himself, Beaton's overwhelming reaction was one of stagestruck awe. "As mementoes of the honour there were a hundred negatives," Beaton recalled, "but in my pocket was hidden, scented with tuberoses and gardenias, a handkerchief that the Queen had tucked behind the cushion of a chair. I had stolen it. It was my particular prize, one which would have more romance and reality than any of the photographs I had taken."

Her Majesty Queen Elizabeth The Queen Mother, 1948.

Photograph by Erwin Blumenfeld, 1938.

THE WAR YEARS

After the German occupation of Prague and the invasion of Poland in August 1939, Britain declared war on Germany. Britain's formal entry into war had become inevitable, yet while for some it was an opportunity to prove themselves, for Beaton it was a numbing blow of anxiety. By September, at a time when his contemporaries were flocking to join the various regiments, Beaton remained at Ashcombe, his house in Wiltshire. "I feel frustrated and ashamed," he wrote in his diary.

This war, as far as I can see, is something specifically designed to show up my inadequacy in every possible capacity. I am too incompetent to enlist as a private in the army. It's doubtful I'd be much good at camouflage. In any case my repeated requests to join have met with, "You'll be called if you're wanted." What else can I do? I have tried all sorts of voluntary jobs in the neighbourhood, helping organize food control, and the distribution of trainloads of refugee children from Whitechapel. I failed in a first aid examination after attending a course given by a humourous and kindly doctor in Salisbury. Now I start as a night telephonist at the Air Raid Precaution centre in Wilton.

Blackouts, restrictions, and shortages of every kind provided constant irritation to the British, but apart from the hardship of an unusually severe winter, little occurred to convince anyone that a second world war was imminent. For months the "Phony War," as it was known, dragged on, until in May 1940 Holland, Belgium, and Luxembourg were invaded in rapid succession.

Surprisingly, only a few days afterward, Beaton's main concern was whether or not to go to America on a commercial assignment. Against his patriotic feelings was set financial need, for Beaton had always spent money easily. Although he intended to leave at a time when British troops were already stationed and fighting in France, his papers were cleared by the Home Office and he left for America with a self-imposed limit of a six-week trip.

Beaton was greeted in New York by friends carrying papers covering the news of the British retreat from Dunkirk. In the midst of work on commercial

Self-portrait with Lord Louis Mountbatten, 1940.

assignments, Beaton kept a close eye on the events and by the time he was free to return to England, he was overwhelmed with guilt.

Beaton arrived back at Southampton, filled with patriotic emotion, and after concerted lobbying by his friends, he at last secured an appointment that had some relation to his talent. Assigned to the Ministry of Information, he was given orders to take pictures of "everything," the results to be used for news and propaganda purposes. By the time the photographs had been shuffled through committees, and cropped and rearranged by various art departments, they were virtually indistinguishable, but they gave Beaton invaluable experience in shooting pictures quickly and instinctively.

Up to this point, Beaton's work had become increasingly isolated, and from the early twenties through the thirties, few pictures were taken outside of his studio or the houses of the rich and famous. His work for the Ministry of Information brought him into an arena of everyday people, and in this environment he began to look at things in an unfussy and almost naïve manner.

London bomb damage, 1940.

As the bombing of London was stepped up, Beaton was given ample fodder for his camera. His first war photographs were of the remains of a factory where three hundred women and girls had been killed when air raid sirens failed to go off. By the end of August nearly every day saw the destruction of buildings both ordinary and historic, and people were forced to stay off the streets, sleep in basements, and follow complicated blackout procedures.

Every day during the bombing of London, Beaton photographed the debris. He recorded in his diary the following not atypical event:

> I went to Albemarle St. to see if the wax head I had seen among the debris of a former hairdressing establishment was still there. As I arrived a demolition squad was pulling down a large top-heavy facade. *Whrump!* The cloud of black dust eventually settled. I clambered over the rubble to find a new wax head lying, bald but still smiling, among the cracked mirrors, glass fragments, and wreckage of the ladies' beauty shop. The men working on the job were helpful, and when I asked one if he had seen the head with the golden hair flying wild, he said he thought that it could be unearthed. It was. The ghoulish head was produced from a mound of rubbish, and I proceeded to photograph it against the dreadful surroundings.
>
> Suddenly the usual officious passerby appeared. A little man with ferret eyes and a pointed red nose. I must show my papers. Yes, there was nothing wrong with the papers, but it didn't say you could photo-

graph those wax heads—it wasn't right—the Ministry of Information would not want to show anything like that. I explained that in any case, my photographs had to be submitted to the censor. But the discontent had started to gather momentum. The newspaper seller, who before had been so blithe and friendly, became truculent and grumbled that he wouldn't let me leave the spot until a policeman appeared and proved that everything was in order. A plain-clothes man edged his way through the gathering crowd and whispered that everything was straightforward but that the feelings of the crowd must be pacified.

> It was some time before the constable appeared and I was escorted to the nearest police station. After a few telephone calls everything was put right, but the constable explained that I had done wrong in provoking the antagonism of the crowd, and a record should be made of the case. This seemed a somewhat empty formality since all the other records had been destroyed by last night's bomb.

Beaton's work for the Ministry of Information served two specific purposes: to document the destruction in London and to reveal to people abroad the reality of what was happening. His most famous single image—that of a young child sitting up in her hospital bed with a bandaged head and rag doll—appeared in magazines and newspapers throughout the world and was credited with gaining massive support for Britain on its American publication.

Beaton's finest work was done, however, when he was able to add his own personal touch without distracting from the gravity of his subject. The pictures of bomb-damaged churches and historic buildings revealed not only the destruction but the grandeur that still existed in the structure of the crumbling walls. The photographs showing the effect of war on the country's domestic population conveyed the tense and alienated atmosphere with such precision that the reality appeared almost staged.

The scenes of children caught unaware by the blackout, of the Princess Royal giving eye tests in the Women's Army, and of the country house with paintings hanging on the walls shrouded by sheets were among Beaton's greatest if less acknowledged pictures. They marked an important milestone in his career, showing that in his photographs it was his vision, not the subject matter, that was dominant. Thematically, the effects of war could not have been further from Beaton's choice of subject, but the moments he chose to record, while unusual and full of an ironic sense of the absurd, conveyed exactly the

War orphans at Wilton, 1940.

alienation he felt. Furthermore, they never failed to take their subject seriously.

In 1941, after a year of photographing London, Beaton was assigned to photograph RAF operations in England. As he traveled through the country, stopping briefly at bases and training schools to take pictures of the young men who made up the country's defense, it dawned on Beaton that he was no longer a part of the younger generation. After flying at 5000 feet to photograph a pilot in his DeHavilland, Beaton revealed to his diary:

> Traveling thus, the wind blew the eyelashes into my eyes, and it was difficult to focus.

> Suddenly, I saw myself reflected in the viewfinder of my camera. The crow's feet around my eyes were those of an old man. Oh, God! Was there no escape from oneself even under these unusual conditions?

The only solace he found was in work, and as he adapted to his new lifestyle, he found he was able to keep his self-centered worries under control. Removed from the rarefied atmosphere of artistic circles, Beaton now dined in the mess with officers whose approval he anxiously sought. When he succeeded in gaining their respect, his confidence expanded, and for the snob from Cambridge and

DeHavilland fighter, 1941.

dandy of London, the experience was once again an education beyond his previously narrow boundaries.

In 1942, anxious to be of greater service, and after a second extensive petitioning of his friends, Beaton was posted to Cairo. On arrival he was immediately presented with the problem of what to wear to comply with military protocol. The Ministry of Information was baffled. British headquarters in Cairo were reluctant to make him an officer but feared that in civilian clothes he might be captured and shot as a spy. After much discussion it was decided that he should wear a Royal Air Force uniform with an embroidered badge reading "Official Photographer" on the shoulder. The uniform delighted Beaton, yet as he sauntered out on a tentative trial of his new clothes, he was aware of eyes trained not on his face but on various parts of his body—his costume consisted of a variety of garments individually appropriate to a senior officer or private but totally meaningless in combination.

Nevertheless, after the austerity of England, the warmth of Egypt and the abundance of supplies were a luxurious change. Beaton's first orders were to photograph "might." He was not to photograph one plane but sixty; never four tanks but a hundred. It was propaganda on a grand scale, yet it held little excitement for Beaton. He had come to the desert to be closer to the war, but the colonial atmosphere and exotic surroundings made the experience seem more like tourism.

Beaton rose early every morning, was ferried to the desert to photograph troop life, and then returned to his Cairo office to develop, sort, and caption his pictures. After two months the pictures he had accumulated numbered in the thousands, but his repeated requests to have the photographs sent on to England were often met with nothing but excuses. The situation augured the beginning of a frustration that was to continue throughout the war, but Beaton carried on with his photography. During his desert excursions, he developed one remarkable sequence of pictures of the skeletal remains of abandoned aircraft. In these pictures Beaton showed his subject as abstract shape and form—a new visualization for him, but, once perceived, one that was never again left unconsidered.

In July 1942, with the German capture of Tobruk and the possibility of an advance on Cairo, Beaton was ordered back to England. He had become too valuable a public relations asset to leave in any danger and was shuttled by a long and circuitous route to London. In the disorienting limbo of travel, Beaton reviewed his status harshly in his diary:

There is much about which to feel dissatisfied. Perhaps it is my greatest mistake to have spent so much time taking photographs. For while I derive satisfaction from taking almost any sort of photograph, nevertheless I realize that only certain compartments of my mind are at work while dabbling with the camera, and this will find me out in the long run. Chunks of my brain matter will have become petrified. Even when taking photographs one must use one's intelligence. A lot of my work could have been taken by automatic pilot.

Although Beaton was dogged perpetually by a feeling that photography could satisfy only part of his potential, he never stopped taking pictures. Within a week of his return, he was photographing the King and Queen with the visiting Mrs. Franklin D. Roosevelt. In December 1943 he received word that the Ministry of Information was ready to send him on another photographic assignment, this time to the Far East. He traveled to India, China, and Burma, narrowly avoiding death when the Dakota in which he was flying was forced to make an emergency landing and blew up within seconds of the passengers' evacuation.

When he finally arrived in Burma, Beaton found that his appearance in civilian clothes had such a morale-boosting effect on men who had seen nothing but khaki uniforms for four years that he was forced to go out photographing in a heavy tweed suit. With almost predictable fluency, though, Beaton mastered yet another genre of picture taking—photojournalism—and his Far Eastern pictures were his first to record events in the direct manner of the traditional war photographer. As distinct from his previous war pictures, the photographs of 1944 were not set pieces but images caught on the run—scenes of hospital operations, fighting, and troop life.

What was most remarkable about these pictures was the range of which they showed Beaton capable. From a portrait and fashion photographer, he had stretched his capacity to include an expertise in modes reaching both ends of the photographic spectrum, yet his pictures never borrowed or imitated from others. In spite of his aversion to taking pictures on "automatic pilot," his instinctive reflex was perhaps his greatest strength, enabling him to use the camera without premeditation to record what he felt.

As his tour of the Far East ended, Beaton once again found his film almost entirely "mislaid." In the summer of 1944, with the war drawing to a close, Beaton gratefully took the opportunity to withdraw from the front, disheartened and disappointed by the vast number of people who had let him down in his efforts to get his pictures back to England. For someone who had so obviously had to push himself to the limit to adapt his whole way of being to the service of his country, the disillusion was doubly felt, and once finished with his work in Burma, Beaton waited only for the opportunity to get to New York, the closest haven.

After a week in Karachi the necessary clearance was obtained. On arrival in New York Beaton was met with the news that his friend Rex Whistler had died in action. Beaton's nerves snapped and he broke down in tears. Barely a week later word came of the liberation of Paris, and for Beaton the war was over.

Remains of tank, Sidi Rezegh, 1942.

In the Libyan Desert, 1942.

"The New Reality," 1946.

"THE NEW REALITY"

By gradual degrees Beaton resumed his transatlantic existence. Once again he was attracted by the lure of theater design, but for financial and temperamental reasons photography took precedence. Still under contract to *Vogue*, Beaton spent most of 1946 in New York, creating a series of pictures of models dressed in high style but posed in attitudes of everyday life—women sewing or hatcheck girls sitting disconsolately in their booths.

Rushed into print and dubbed "The New Reality," the pictures were an immediate success, but the implication behind the title—that the war had brought about a markedly different way of seeing—was misleading. Although Beaton himself had matured into a more rounded and open person, the photographs were simply a progression of his work of the thirties. Nevertheless, it was with these pictures that Beaton enjoyed his greatest success, and the period in which he photographed in this manner was for him one of the most secure in his life.

Adding to his happiness, in March 1946, Beaton effected his first reunion with Greta Garbo. Straining to pick up the strands of what he instinctively felt was an uncommon relationship, he threw himself at her without caution. To his great surprise, his advances were reciprocated, and barely a month later Beaton proposed marriage. His offer was rejected as unrealistic, but they continued to see each other every day, shopping together, taking long walks in Central Park, and indulging in all the superficial pursuits of lovers.

Well aware of Garbo's hatred of all forms of publicity, Beaton reluctantly put aside all thoughts of photographing her, and the only time he was invited to take her picture was when Garbo needed a new passport photograph. The resulting pictures revealed a face still beautiful but consumed by its own concerns.

The relationship between Beaton and Garbo was a complex affair: Beaton was head over heels in love, while Garbo vacillated between commitment and indifference. They would see each other daily, and then Garbo would go away for a month, refusing to answer Beaton's calls. In spite of the callous way he was sometimes treated, Beaton was profoundly at peace with himself. As he wrote in his diary:

At this juncture I am able to derive much satisfaction from my career, realizing that life can be satisfying without all that one wants.

After a sluggish start, my creative efforts seem to have built up a force that is pulling me forward with excitement, but it is not work for work's sake, or money, or even fulfilling some of the ambitions formed at Cambridge. It is more a feeling of achieving substance.

Being seen with Garbo and being known as her most frequent companion were a source of great pride to Beaton, but eventually the relationship began to take its toll on Beaton's energy. Although he was aware that he should have countered Garbo's insensitivity with a display of his own nonchalance, Beaton was unable to change his own course of action. The diaries that chronicled the most intense years of their relationship were tellingly titled first *The Happy Years* (1944–1948), then *The Strenuous Years* (1948–1955). By the early 1950s, reflecting once more on his career, Beaton wrote:

I do not want to go back to my old vomit. Enough of taking fashions on young models who survive just as long as their faces show no signs of character, or of elderly but rich harpies appearing as if butter would not melt in their terrible mouths.

I cannot give up photography: it is an important part of my life, but perhaps I can be strong enough to turn down photographic offers that are no longer a challenge.

After many years of pursuing Garbo and neglecting his own work, Beaton was finally prepared to reverse his priorities. Yet at the very time he was realizing a more purist attitude toward his work, the trend of fashion was conspiring to thwart him.

With photographers like Richard Avedon and Irving Penn moving to the forefront of their medium, for the first time in his career Beaton began to appear old-fashioned. As he churned out pictures according to old formulas, the demand for his services diminished. The aesthetic changes that were replac-

Photograph by Compton Collier, 1951.

editor, Edna Chase, he would have lost his job long before. He was temperamental, he threw scenes, and the other editors could not abide working with him.

What Myers said rang true enough for Beaton to realize that it was not malicious gossip. Furthermore, it was obvious that Myers had acted in Beaton's best interest in telling him what he had heard. Beaton's only solace came from Diana Vreeland, then editor of *Harper's Bazaar*. "Perhaps you're moving through a subterranean passage and haven't yet come out to the light," she told him, "but you will, Cecil, you will! Mark my words."

Before matters improved, however, they got worse. Within a year Beaton's contract with *Vogue* was terminated. His main source of income disappeared, and he was faced with the prospect of re-establishing himself.

As Beaton entered his fifties, his interests and the choice of his photographic subjects began to change. In 1956 he had been given fresh employment in New York by *Harper's Bazaar,* and in rooms at the Ambassador Hotel decorated to his specifications, he photographed a procession of personalities sent to him by the magazine. Marilyn Monroe, Hermione Gingold, and Carson McCullers all posed against the distinctive dotted design of the suite, yet as repetitive and restated as this background was, the portraits taken against it have a strength that comes from Beaton's depth of understanding of each character.

In 1976 I asked Beaton how he thought his own portraiture had changed through the years. He replied that at the beginning it had been the person's aura that had interested him, while later it had been the person. These later pictures prove the statement's validity. The weariness of Monroe's face and pose and the self-deprecating humor of Gingold were impressions that reached past the superficialities of their public image.

By 1957 the typical Beaton subject was no longer a smart young thing seen in all his or her finery, but a study of the effects of age on beauty, or the changes wrought by experience on the faces of the personalities of a generation. As Beaton reverted to the naïve approach of his war photography, his portraits became once again virtual snapshots. Their candidness revealed their subjects not as a photographer might see them in his studio, but as they appeared to him in life—Evelyn Waugh, smugly self-satisfied, posing behind a fence marked *"Entrée interdite aux promeneurs"*; Bernard Berenson holding himself erect with dignity, against a brilliant shaft of sunlight. In all the photographs of this period, the direct composition of Beaton's earliest pictures fills the frame, the abstract shape of light and shade as effective and powerful as the subjects themselves.

ing the theatricality of Beaton's work—Avedon's rugged, energetic, and relentless vision, and Penn's graceful and articulate composition—were seized on by the magazines. As if to underline his failure to meet the challenge of this new sensibility, Beaton returned to the one field where convention and unchangeability were valued most—photographing royalty.

Beaton's photographs of the Royal Family were a marked improvement over the standard of the genre. He showed mood and personality instead of the usual seriousness and formality, and several images stand out at once: the young and radiant Queen Elizabeth II in her coronation robes, smiling up at the camera; the pensive beauty of Princess Alexandra. Yet for all their qualities these pictures could have as easily been taken twenty years previously.

For a while Beaton was able to ignore the pressures of impending redundancy, but in 1954 the process of facing reality began when a friend, John Myers, came to see Beaton to tell him of some gossip he had overheard. What he had heard was that Beaton was in a precarious position at *Vogue,* that his work was unpublishable, and that he was no longer allotted space in the magazine. His attitude was that of the 1930s, and were it not for the influence of the

Greta Garbo, 1946.

Audrey Hepburn as My Fair Lady.

Marilyn Monroe, 1956.

Throughout the late fifties and early sixties, Beaton's attention became increasingly taken up with theatrical and cinematic work. He designed the sets and costumes for the films *Gigi* and *My Fair Lady,* winning Oscars for both, and with the time and means to indulge his pleasure, he once again took to travel. Never without a camera, Beaton recorded the sights of his journeys. With no one to please but himself, and freed from all aesthetic restraints, he brought all his experience to bear on these most personal pictures. The results showed scenes not just as an artist would perceive them but as an artist with a camera would. His subjects were often aware of the camera, his perspective was often exaggeratedly photographic, but the knowledge of this adds to rather than intrudes on the pictures. Flour sifters in Bangkok are revealed peering through the powder that surrounds them every day. A Moroccan beggar girl is shown from a vantage point that reflects the emotional and intellectual distance between photographer and subject. In terms of presenting images in the particular context of their medium, these pictures, like Beaton's earlier pictures of New York, were years ahead of their time, but with no conve-

Photographing The Queen Mother, Princess Anne, and Prince Charles on Coronation Day, 1953.

nient place to exhibit them, they were left in Beaton's files and ignored by Beaton himself for their very nonconformity.

With the advent of the sixties, Beaton was at last able to feel that he was moving into an epoch in sympathy with his own inclinations, and in contrast to the conservative ethic of the previous decade, he was electrified by the youthfulness of the new era. He was soon on familiar terms with Mick Jagger and the Rolling Stones, David Hockney, and Rudolf Nureyev, and while some were to see this as a rather forced camaraderie, in reality Beaton was among the very first to see and appreciate the talents of these individuals. Without being faddish or unconditionally

approving, Beaton was simply eager to learn from a generation that he recognized as so different from his own. On Jagger's advice, Beaton went so far as to try LSD several times, taking the drug with, in his own words, "much pleasure and success."

In the sixties and early seventies, as one contemporary after another passed away, Beaton found the necessity of staying modern weighing heavily against a feeling of anachronism. A series of experiments with multiple exposures resulted in a repetitive and unexciting book titled *Images.* With the exception of his portraiture, for the most part Beaton's work stood still. In 1971 his sister Baba died. The only happiness the year brought was the surprise an-

W. H. Auden, 1954.

Mick Jagger, 1967.

nouncement of a knighthood, and with the title, Sir Cecil, Beaton reluctantly accepted that he had become one of the respected elders of photography.

In 1973 Beaton wrote in his diary:

> Am really sorry for myself. So far I've enjoyed more than average good health, but lately a blight has been put on my existence by my not being able to use my eyes without being punished by a nervous head pain. It puts such a damper on my activities. I live by my eyes.

With his photographic activity limited, Beaton allowed the responsibility of organizing and displaying his work to pass on to others. In 1974 he presided over an exhibition of his war photography at the Imperial War Museum in London. It was a proud but upsetting experience, for, as Beaton put it, "I felt that I was dead and that people were speaking of me in the past."

Ironically, in July 1974, just after Beaton had resolved to continue his life energetically, he suffered a severe stroke. His right side was paralyzed, and prolonged speech or activity became increasingly difficult. Recovering at his home in Wiltshire, Beaton decided to sell his entire photographic output, and in February 1977 Sotheby's Belgravia bought and took possession of a row of filing cabinets containing more than 150,000 photographs, a quarter of a million negatives, countless color transparencies, and more than a dozen scrapbooks.

The sale seemed to signify the final phase of Beaton's career, but with astonishing resilience, by 1979, Beaton was photographing again. At first the pictures he took were somewhat restrained, his spontaneity hampered by the need to use a tripod at all times, but as he persevered, his self-assurance and individuality returned.

On my last visit to Sir Cecil in the Autumn of 1979, his photographs of the Paris collections had just appeared over a thirty-page spread in French *Vogue,* and with the activity his energy and curiosity appeared to have revived. On January 14, he celebrated his seventy-sixth birthday. On January 17, excusing himself, Sir Cecil went to bed early. He died peacefully in his sleep on the morning of January 18.

Beaton's studio, photographed by Conrad Hafenrichter.

BEATON

The Plates

Nancy and Baba Beaton, 1915.

Nancy and Baba, with their friend Esther Middleton, 1916.

Baba, 1922.

Nancy, 1926.

Baba, 1926.

Baba, 1925.

Baba, 1925.

Nancy, 1926.

Baba, Wanda Baillie-Hamilton, and Lady Bridget Poullett, 1928.

Georgia (Mrs. Sacheverell) Sitwell, 1927.

William Walton, 1926.

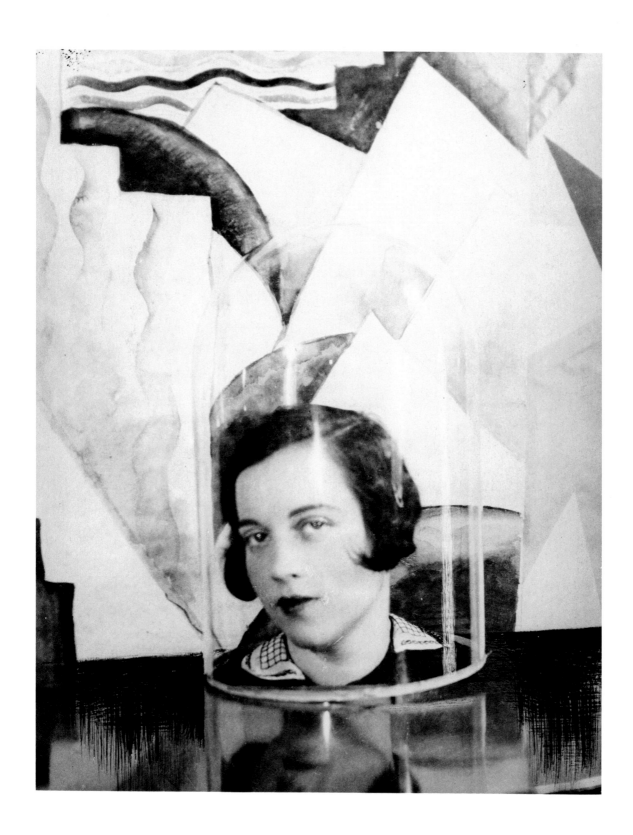

Lady Milbanke, 1927.

Lady Oxford, 1927.

68

Sacheverell Sitwell, 1927.

The Dashwood family, 1926.

Edith Sitwell, 1927.

Edith Sitwell, 1927.

Paula Gellibrand, 1928.

Tilly Losch, 1929.

Gwili André, 1931.

Gary Cooper, 1931.

Johnny Weissmuller, 1931.

Dolores Del Rio, 1931.

Katharine Hepburn, 1934.

Orson Welles, 1934.

Buster Keaton, 1931.

Carole Lombard, 1931.

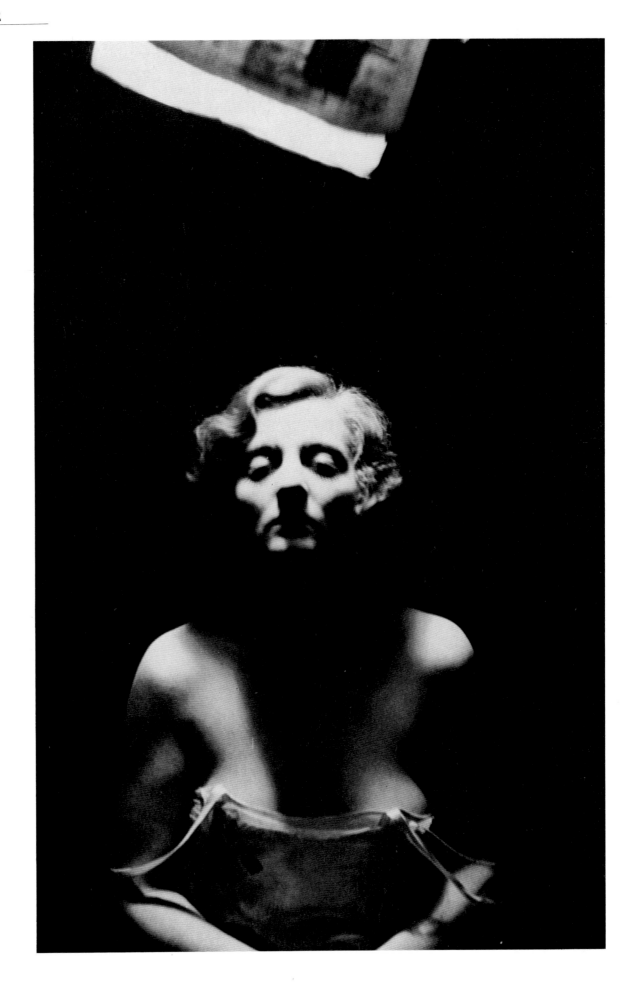

Tallulah Bankhead, 1931.

Marlene Dietrich, 1930.

Alice White, 1931.

John Wayne, 1931.

Lady Ursula Manners, 1937.

Lady Diana Cooper, 1932.

Mrs. Reginald Fellowes, 1931.

Nancy Cunard, 1927.

Laurence Olivier as Romeo, 1935.

John Gielgud as Mercutio, 1935.

92

Miss Eileen Agar, 1927.

Mrs. Shevlin Smith, 1936.

Gertrude Lawrence, 1928.

Gertrude Lawrence, 1930.

Rosamond Pinchot, 1930.

Phyllis Calvert, 1939.

Danilova, 1937.

Olga Lynn, 1934.

Aldous Huxley, 1936.

Salvador and Gala Dali, 1936.

Lady Diana Cooper, 1930.

Norma Shearer, 1930.

Mrs. Harrison Williams, 1937.

Natasha Paley, 1936.

Mrs. Shevlin Smith, 1936.

Carol Reed, 1940.

Robinson Jeffers, 1931.

Serge Lifar, 1938.

Giorgio de Chirico, 1936.

Jean Cocteau, 1932.

General Charles de Gaulle, 1941.

Winston Churchill, 1940.

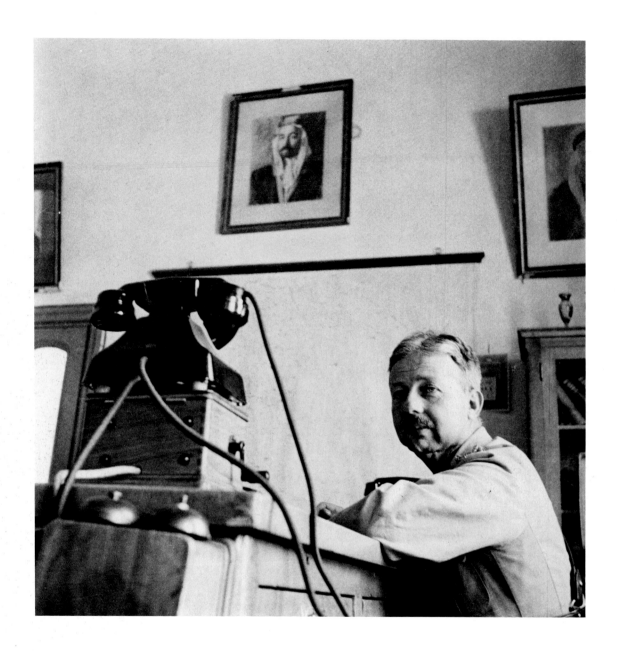

Glubb Pasha, 1942.

Winston Churchill and General de Gaulle, 1941.

General Dwight D. Eisenhower, 1943.

General Carton de Wiart, 1943.

Lord Halifax, 1940.

Churchill's bedroom, 10 Downing Street, 1940.

Lady Anglesey and Lady Caroline Paget, at Plas Newydd, Wales, 1940.

Beistigui House, outside Paris. Left to right: *Charles Beistigui, Denise Bourdet, and Lady Abdy, 1941.*

London bomb damage, 1940.

Bomb damage and survivors, 1940.

Princess Mary, the Princess Royal, 1940.

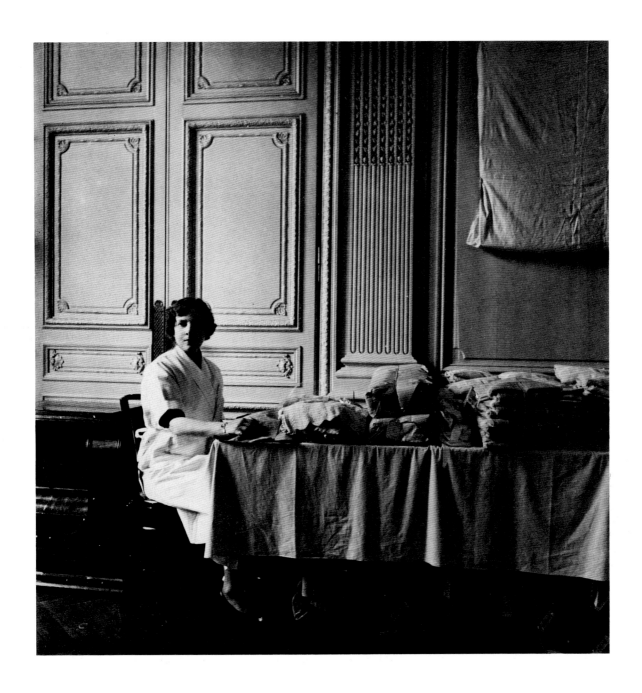

Lady Maud Carnegie at home, 1940

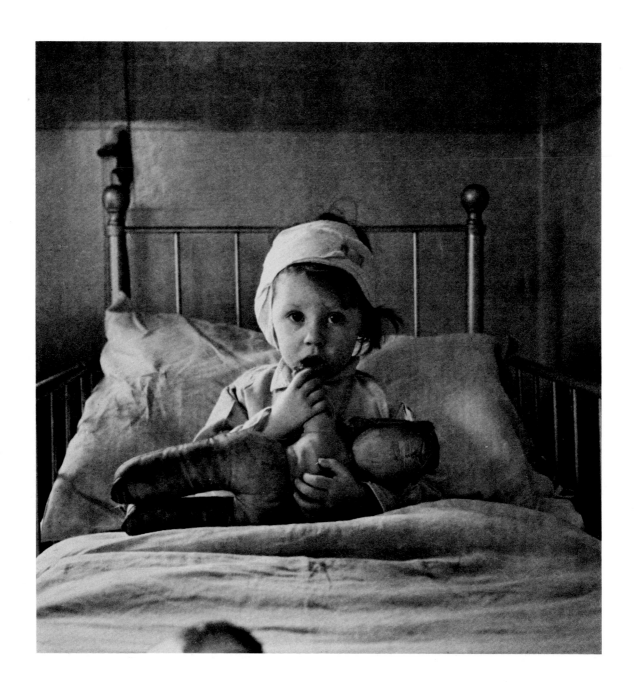

London bomb victim, 1940.

Evacuated children during a blackout, 1940.

Beistigui House, 1941

London bomb damage: St. Paul's Cathedral, 1940.

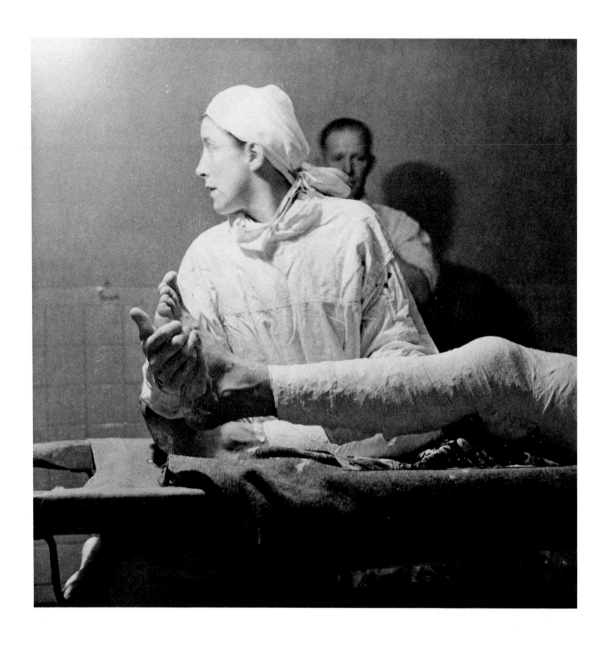

Field hospital, Libyan Desert, 1942.

Bombed fire station, Tobruk, 1942.

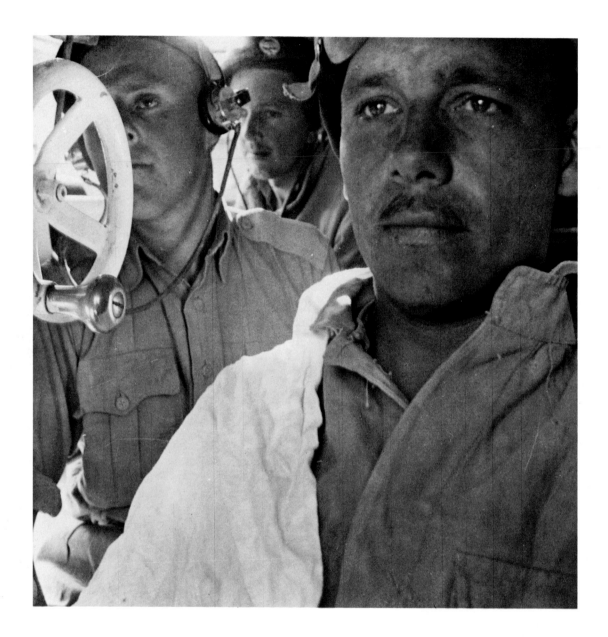

Eighth Army tank crew, 1942.

Sandstorm in the Libyan Desert, 1942.

Carrying the wounded, Burma, 1944.

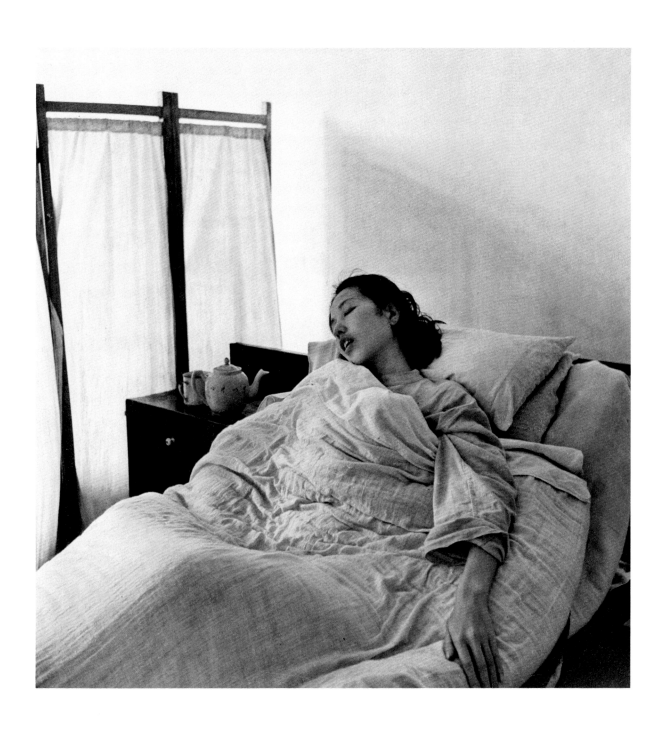

Chinese casualty, Chekiang Province, 1944.

Sleeping figures, Calcutta, 1943.

Off-duty sailor, 1944.

Chinese soldier, 1944.

Chinese Military Police, 1945.

Burnt-out aircraft, Libyan Desert, 1942.

Burnt-out aircraft, Libyan Desert, 1942.

Pablo Picasso, 1945.

Jean Cocteau, 1945.

Gertrude Stein, 1945.

Mr. and Mrs. Randolph Churchill, 1953.

Greta Garbo, 1946.

Greta Garbo, 1946.

Greta Garbo, 1946.

Greta Garbo, 1946.

Cole Porter, 1953.

W. H. Auden, 1954.

Carson McCullers, 1956.

Noel Coward, 1943.

Marlon Brando, 1947.

Augustus John, 1940.

Grace Kelly, 1954.

Judy Garland, 1953.

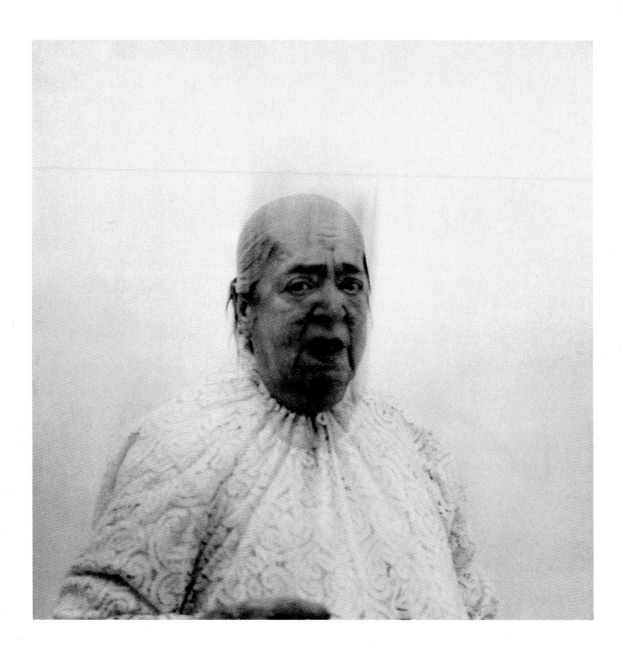

Elsa Maxwell, 1960.

Evelyn Waugh, 1957.

Marilyn Monroe, 1956.

Hermione Gingold, 1956.

162

Raoul Dufy, 1945.

Augustus John and family, 1960.

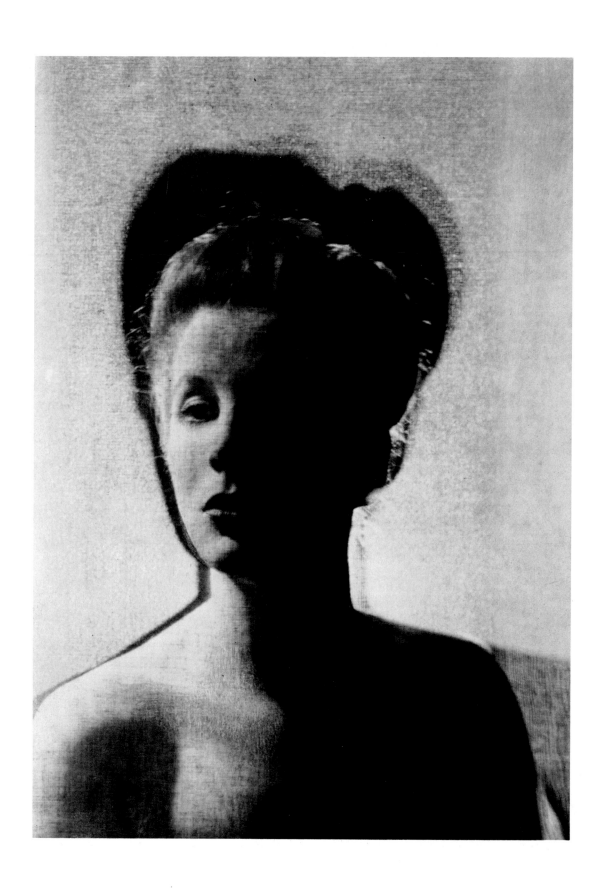

Diana Wynyard, 1947.

Leopold Stokowski, 1957.

T. S. Eliot, 1956.

Igor Stravinsky, 1956.

Contessa Romanones, 1958.

Marianne Moore and her mother, 1950.

Graham Sutherland with his portrait of Somerset Maugham, 1949.

Walter Sickert and his wife, 1940.

Bernard Berenson, 1957.

J. Krishnamurti, 1959.

Mexico, 1931.

New York, 1940.

New York, 1937.

New York, 1937.

New York, 1937.

New York, 1937

Morocco, 1937.

Morocco, 1937.

Morocco, 1958.

Bangkok flour factory, 1957.

Morocco, 1958.

Morocco, 1959.

Charlotte Brontë's dress, Haworth, 1957.

Corsica, 1938.

Spain, 1960.

Spain, 1960.

Albert Finney, 1960.

Audrey Hepburn, 1958.

Ingrid Bergman, 1958.

Katharine Hepburn, 1969.

Jeanne Moreau, 1963.

Beyond the Fringe *cast: Peter Cook, Dudley Moore, Alan Bennett, and Jonathan Miller, 1964.*

David Hockney, 1965.

...ien Freud, 1956.

Rudolf Nureyev, 1963.

Truman Capote, 1950.

Kin Hoitsma, 1964.

Richards, 1967.

Pavlova's death mask, 1960.

Lady Caroline and Joanna Cholmondeley, 1971.

Lucien Freud's daughter, 1956.

Mae Murray, star of silent films, 1962.

The Earl of Harewood, 1968.

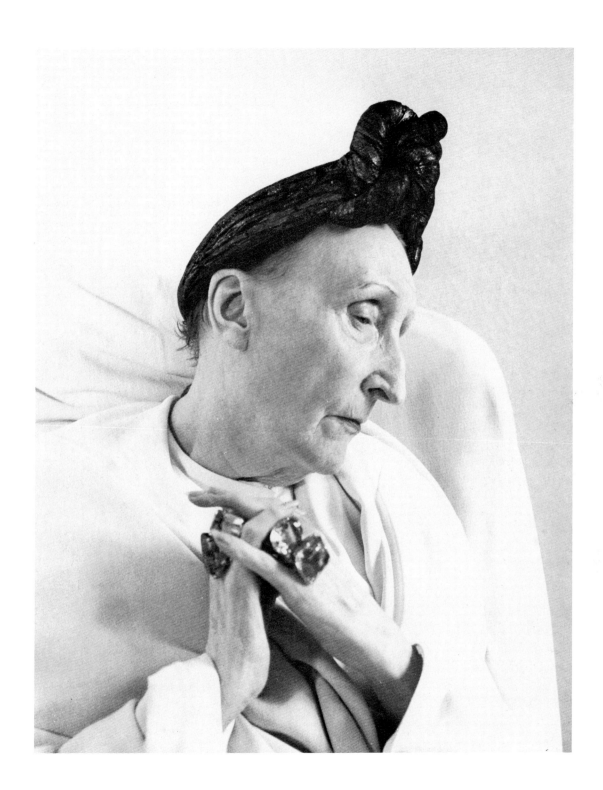

Edith Sitwell, 1962.

Fashion, 1929.

Mariana Van Rensselaer in a Charles James hat, 1930.

New York fashion, 1930.

Fashion, 1934.

Fashion, 1939.

Fashion, 1937.

Fashion, 1951.

Fashion, 1939.

Fashion, 1938.

Fashion, 1941.

Paris fashion, 1946.

Fashion, 1949.

Fashion, 1946.

Fashion, 1939.

Schiaparelli hats, 1936.

Fashion, 1948.

Charles James evening dresses, 1948.

Fifties fashion.

Fashion, 1958.

228

Jean Shrimpton, 1966.

Jean Shrimpton, 1966.

Paris Fashion, 1979.

Paris Fashion, 1979.

King Edward VIII, 1937.

The Duchess of Windsor, 1937.

234

The Duke and Duchess of Windsor at the Château de Candé, 1937.

Her Majesty Queen Elizabeth The Queen Mother, 1948.

Her Majesty The Queen, Coronation Day, 1953.

Her Royal Highness Princess Anne, Coronation Day, 1953.

Her Royal Highness Princess Alexandra, 1958.

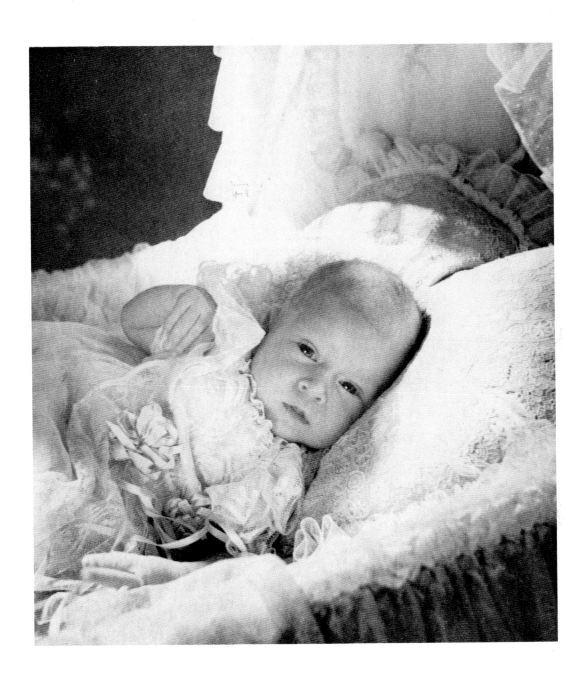

His Royal Highness Prince Charles, 1948.

Her Majesty The Queen, 1945.

Her Majesty The Queen, Coronation Day, 1953.

Her Majesty The Queen, 1955.

Her Majesty The Queen, 1968.

Lady Jersey, 1929.

Tilly Losch, 1934.

Rex Harrison and Lilli Palmer with their son, 1953.

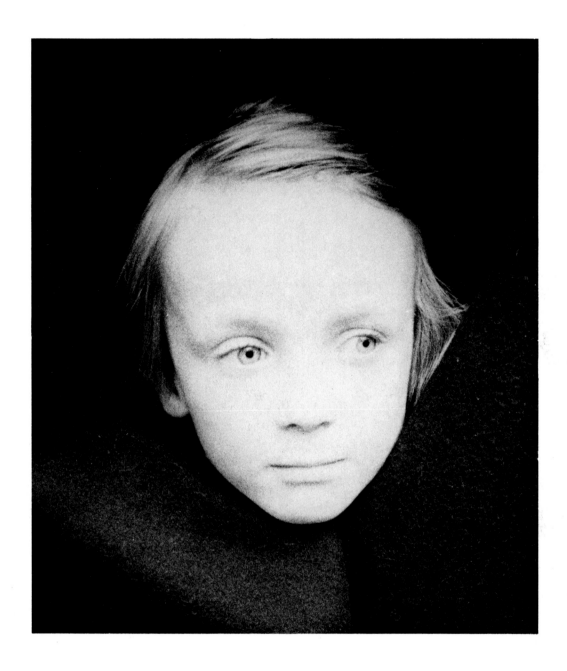

Alexander Quennell, 1973.

Lady Caroline Paget, 1937.

England, 1954.

250

From Images, *1963.*

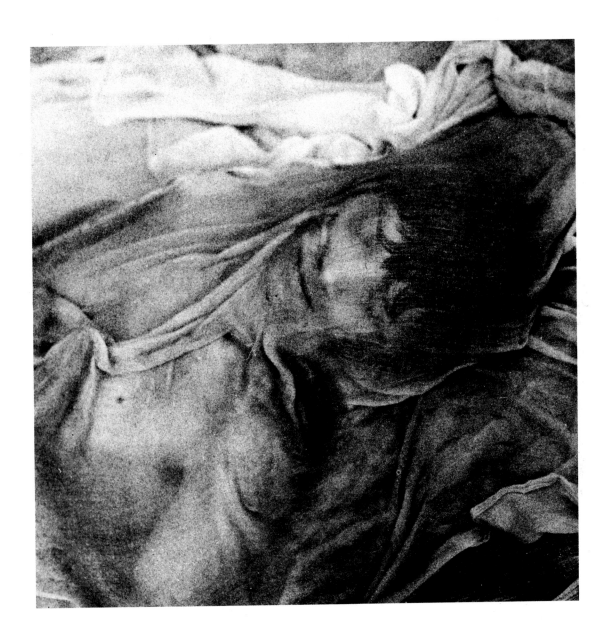

Gervase, 1970.

Mrs. J. J. Astor's cat, 1971.

Lord Berners, Ashcombe, 1937.

INDEX

(Figures in italics indicate illustrations)

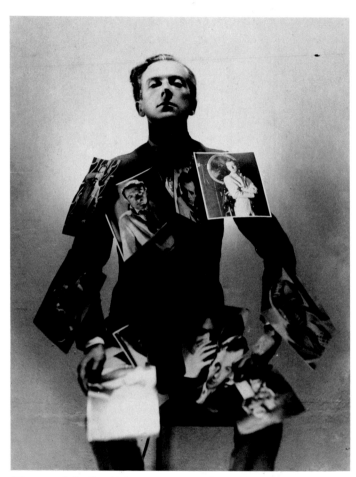

Photograph by Paul Tanqueray, 1933.